ARENA
POCKET
GUIDE

INTERMEDIATE
Western
Exercises

CHERRY HILL

STOREY
BOOKS

The mission of Storey Publishing is to serve our customers by publishing practical information that encourages personal independence in harmony with the environment.

Edited by Deborah Burns and Aimee Poirier
Cover design by Eugenie Delaney
Cover photographs by Richard Klimesh
Text design by Cindy McFarland
Production assistance by Susan Bernier and Jen Jepson
Line drawings designed by Cherry Hill and drawn
  by Peggy Judy

The information in this book is true and complete to the best of our knowledge. All recommendations are made without guarantee on the part of the author or Storey Publishing. The author and publisher disclaim any liability in connection with the use of this information. For additional information please contact Storey Books, 210 MASS MoCA Way, North Adams, MA 01247.

Storey books are available for special premium and promotional uses and for customized editions. For further information, please call the Custom Publishing Department at 800-793-9396.

Printed in Canada by Transcontinental Printing
10 9 8 7 6 5 4 3

Library of Congress Cataloging-in-Publication Data

Hill, Cherry, 1947–
    Intermediate western exercises / by Cherry Hill.
        p.   cm. — (Arena pocket guide)
    ISBN 1-58017-046-3 (pbk. : alk. paper)
    1. Western horses — Training. 2. Western riding. I. Title.
    II. Series: Hill, Cherry, 1947– Arena pocket guide.
    SF309.34.H57 1998
    798.2'3—dc21   97-49046
                                                                          CIP

Intermediate Western Exercises

Arena exercises are a cross between gymnastics, meditation, and geometry. They are essential keys for discovering many important principles about training and riding.

Goals
- Hone balance and precise use of aids
- Improve bending
    Half turns
    Serpentines
- Tighten transitions
    Lope to walk, walk to lope
    Simple lead changes
- Develop lateral work
    Turn on the forehand
    Western two-step
    Hindquarter pivot
- Begin collection
    The back
    The check

Remember as you practice that it is the QUALITY of the work that is most important. It is a much greater accomplishment to do simple things well than it is to stumble through advanced maneuvers in poor form and with erratic rhythm. Keep your mind in the middle and a leg on each side.

How Can You Tell If the Work Is Correct?

1. Work regularly with a qualified instructor.

2. Ask a qualified person to stand on the ground, observe your exercises, and report to you what he or she sees.

3. Have someone record your exercises on videotape. Then watch the tape carefully using slow motion and freeze frame.

4. As you ride, watch yourself and your horse in large mirrors on the wall.

5. Without moving your head, glance down at your horse's shoulders, neck, poll, and eye during different maneuvers to determine if he is correct up front.

6. Ultimately, the key is to develop a *feel* for when things are going right and when they are going wrong by utilizing all of the above feedback techniques. Answer the following by feeling, not looking:

★ Is there appropriate left to right balance on my seat bones? Can I feel them both?

★ Can I feel even contact on both reins?

★ Is the front to rear balance acceptable or is the horse heavy on the forehand, croup up, back hollow?

★ Is the rhythm regular or does the horse speed up, slow down, or break gait?

★ Is my horse relaxed or is his back tense?

★ Is he on the bit or above or behind it?

★ Is my horse loping on the correct lead?

★ Can I tell when his inside hind leg is about to land?

What Do You Do When Things Go Wrong?

1. Review each component of an exercise.

2. You may need to return to some very basic exercises to establish forward movement, acceptance of contact, or response to sideways driving aids. Returning to simple circle work will often improve straightness and subsequently improve lateral work and collection.

3. Ride an exercise that the horse does very well, such as the walk-jog-walk transition. Work on purity and form.

4. Perform a simpler version of the exercise. If it is a lope exercise, try it at a walk or jog first.

5. Perform the exercise in the opposite direction. Sometimes, because of an inherent stiffness or crookedness in a horse, you will have difficulty with an exercise to the left but no problems to the right! Capitalize on this by refining your skills and the application of your aids in the "good" direction and then return to the "hard" direction with a renewed sense of what needs to be done. I often find that doing work to the right improves work to the left.

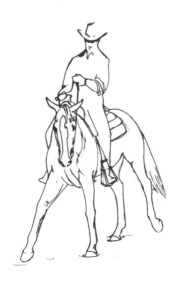

Back

- Always start on a straight line from a square halt.
- Keep even weight on both seat bones, but don't sit real deep. Bear some weight on your thighs without leaning forward.
- Flex your gluteal muscles and abdominals to tilt your pelvis and bring your seat bones forward.
- Straighten your lower back to help your seat bones come forward.
- Apply equal pressure with both legs at the cinch.
- As the horse arrives at the bit, maintain non-allowing equal direct rein pressure to encourage him to let his impulsion out backwards.
- Once the horse has yielded at jaw, poll, and loin, and has begun moving backward, lighten rein aids but maintain contact and continue seat and leg aids.
- To discontinue backing, release rein aids but continue seat and leg aids momentarily to drive the horse up to a halt or a forward gait.

The back is a "man-made" diagonal, two-beat gait in reverse. In nature, horses rarely back up for more than a step or two.

When backing promptly, the left hind and right front are lifted distinctly, moved backward, and placed down together. They alternate with the right hind and left front in a precise synchronization.

When backing more slowly, the diagonal pairs break on landing, the front landing ahead of its diagonal hind.

The back is best ridden when thought of as a "forward" gait because the horse must first be ridden up into contact as if he were going to walk.

* Riding the back is valuable for suppleness, obedience, and developing strength of back and hindquarters of any horse.
* If your horse "gets stuck" or "freezes," use squeeze and release, vibrations, or light alternating reins to untrack him. Never try to *pull* a horse backward.
* If a horse backs too slowly or unwillingly, the back becomes a labored, four-beat gait, and often the horse will drag his feet backward rather than lift his legs.
* If a horse backs crookedly, apply the leg on the side to which he is angling his hindquarters. If he is swinging his hindquarters to the right, first be sure you are not causing it with your left leg or left rein. If they are OK, apply your right leg behind the cinch to straighten him.
* Never start the back with the reins.
* Backing can be overdone and cause anticipation, a dangerous rapid rushing backward, or can cause the horse to use backing as an avoidance behavior.
* A horse needs to become gradually accustomed to the concept of backing, and he must be allowed to build up his coordination and strength before he is asked to back for long distances.

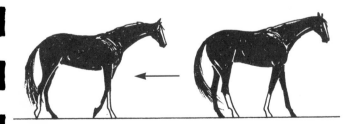

Check

- Jog
- Corner
- Halt
- Jog
- Halt

- Jog
- Check
- Jog
- Check
- Jog

A check is a preparatory set of aids that drives and controls the horse. It is a means of momentarily re-balancing the horse, elevating the forehand, increasing hindquarter engagement, evening an erratic rhythm, slowing a pace, and reminding the horse not to lean on the bit or rush. A check is a momentary holding (a non-allowing in contrast to a pulling or taking), immediately followed by a yielding (within one stride or a split second).

How to Apply a Check

Think. Apply seat, leg, and hand aids. Yield. A check is an almost simultaneous application of the following with an emphasis on the seat and legs, and a de-emphasis on the hands:

★ Keep upper body straight or slightly back with elevated sternum.
★ Maintain deep, still contact of seat bones on saddle from flexed abdominals and a flattened lower back, bringing seat bones forward.
★ Keep both lower legs on horse's side at the cinch.
★ Use an appropriate intensity with both hands. The following is a list in increasing intensity:
  - Close fingers.
  - Squeeze reins.
  - Roll hands inward.
  - Move arm backward from shoulder.
  - Lean upper body back.

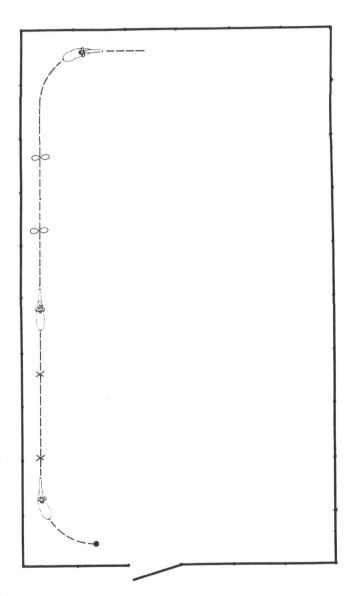

The timing of the yield is crucial. If you wait so long that you can feel the full effects of the check, it is way past time to yield. The yield is what encourages self-carriage. No yield leads to stiffness and tension.

EXERCISE 3

Lope — Walk — Lope

- Jog.
- Lope.
- Lope large circle.
- Three strides before rail, do a series of checks.
- Lope straight one stride.
- Walk, keeping weight on both seat bones and shoulders over hips.
- Walk 1–2 strides.
- Make a slight bend right.
- Use a strong inside leg to outside rein.
- Bend to the inside.
- Hold outside leg.
- Lope right lead in a large circle.
- Continue the sequence.

This exercise develops left-right balance in horse and rider.

- ★ You can align your horse's body more correctly with a walk-lope transition than a jog-lope transition.
- ★ It is easier to teach the walk-lope depart after you have been loping.
- ★ At first, the lope-walk transition might require a few steps of jog. Gradually, you and your horse will develop the balance and coordination to go directly from a lope to a walk.
- ★ Don't lean forward on the upward transition. This would hinder the horse by weighting his forehand.
- ★ Your horse must be on the aids and able to lope in balance before you try the walk-lope transition.
- ★ If the horse is getting behind the bit or taking mincing steps before the lope depart, jog actively forward, then check, walk, and lope.
- ★ If your horse throws his head or inverts his neck, he has had improper preparation and balance.

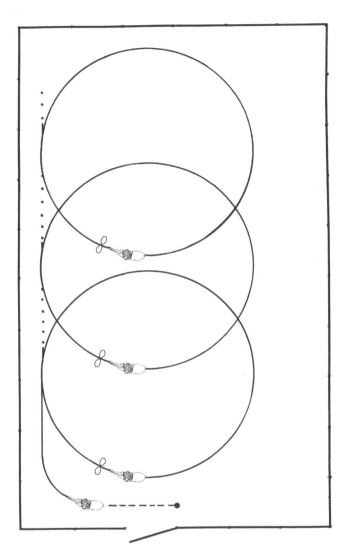

* Using the inside rein too strongly could cause the horse to take the incorrect lead. If already loping, a too-strong inside rein could cause him to break into a jog.
* If your horse breaks into a jog, go back to the walk. Don't push him into a lope from a fast jog.
* Keep your horse up on the outside rein so he won't drop to the inside and become heavy on his leading foreleg. You want him to be light!

Jog — Halt — Back — Walk

- Jog.
- Jog corner.
- When straight, walk.
- Walk 1–2 strides.
- Jog 4–6 strides.
- Halt.
- Jog 4–6 strides.
- Halt, making sure horse yields at the jaw and poll during the transition.
- Back 2 strides.
- Walk.

The suppleness and position of your horse's jaw, poll, and back at the final halt are key to getting fluid back steps without tenseness or resistance.

The entire exercise is to be ridden along the rail. The arena map is "exploded" sideways to show the components that occur on top of each other.

★ Increases engagement of hind legs.
★ This exercise is a barometer of how supple the horse is through the jaw, poll, and back.

Take your time. If you are abrupt with the halts or back, your horse will likely lose form.

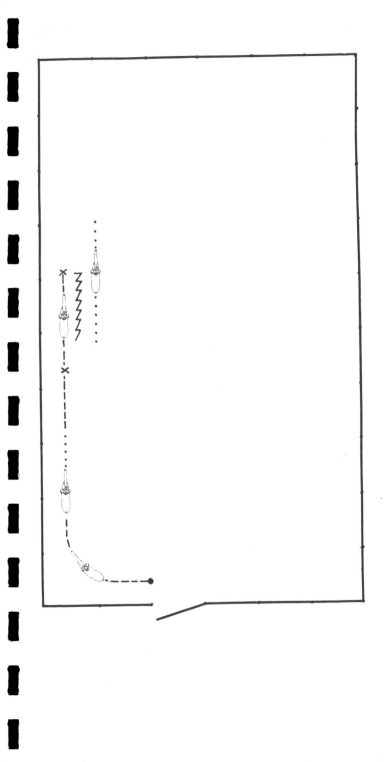

Change of Lead through Jog

- Lope right lead.
- Lope the right corner.
- Lope the long side.
- Lope the right corner.
- In the second corner of the short end, lope a 40-foot circle.
- As you finish the circle, head across long diagonal.
- After loping straight a stride or two, check, sit deep, and jog.
- Move your hands forward to allow the horse to extend the jog.
- As you jog, change your aids so the horse is ready to work to the left.
- Apply aids for lope left lead.
- Lope the corner to the left.
- Lope straight ahead.

★ At first it may take several strides of jog for you to get organized. Eventually, you should lope on the new lead after three steps of jog.

★ Take advantage of the impulsion from the previous lope to give you a good, forward lope in the new direction by not jogging too long.

★ Allows you to change leads when you change direction on a young horse.

★ Allows you to focus on the departs to solidify timing.

Changing leads through a jog is used in some Western horsemanship patterns.

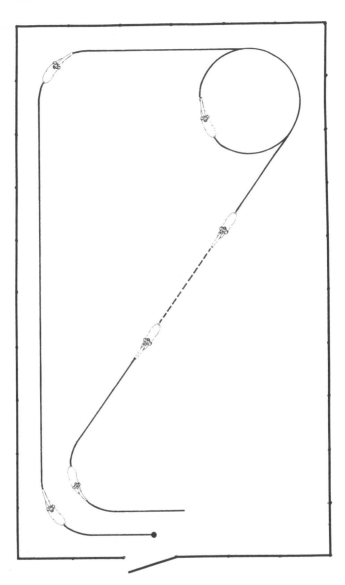

Don't pull backward on the reins, as this creates a backward, hollow transition, with the horse jamming his forehand stiffly on the ground. You need a forward, up-in-front transition to jog so you can readily lope off on the new lead.

Half Turn

Half turn to the right:

- Leave the rail and begin riding a small circle.
- At the widest part of the circle, ride a diagonal line back toward track.
- Initiate left flexion.

Half turn in reverse:

- Leave the rail using mild right bend.
- Straighten and ride a diagonal line until you are about 20 feet from the rail.
- Initiate bend to left.
- Ride a small circle to left.
- Straighten.

Provides a more concise and immediate way to change direction than on a diagonal or figure 8.

Many horses slow down their rhythm in a half turn. This usually occurs for one of two reasons. The young horse decreases his tempo because he interprets increased bit pressure as a signal to slow down. He hasn't learned to differentiate the various pressures on the bit. The horse that is lazy or out-of-condition will slow down because it requires more energy to perform a half turn in balance and at the correct tempo than it does to perform one sloppily. Keep your forward driving aids on your horse so he doesn't lose rhythm in the turn.

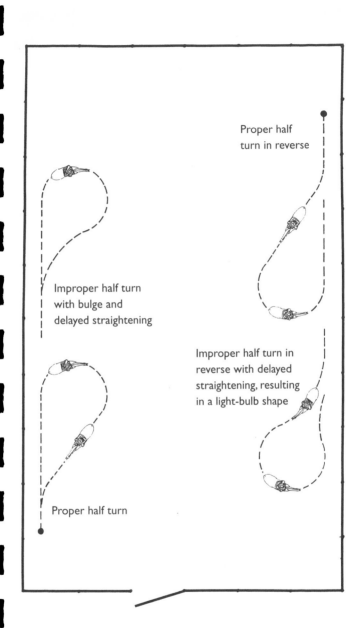

Proper half
turn in reverse

Improper half turn
with bulge and
delayed straightening

Improper half turn in
reverse with delayed
straightening, resulting
in a light-bulb shape

Proper half turn

*A half turn should look more like an ice cream cone
than a tear drop or a light bulb.*

Turn on the Forehand

- Walk.
- Right corner at a walk.
- Drift off the track so you are about 10–15 feet from the rail and have room for the turn.
- Halt.
- Turn on the forehand 180 degrees with left flexion and hindquarters moving to the right.
  - Flex horse's head to the left with a shortened left rein.
  - Weight left seat bone.
  - Use left leg actively behind the cinch to push the hindquarters to the right.
  - Use right leg at the cinch to keep the horse moving in a forward walk rhythm, from rushing sideways to the right, and from backing up.

In a turn on the forehand where the hindquarters move right and the horse is flexed left (as on arena map):
- ★ Footfall pattern is left hind, left front, right hind, right front.
- ★ The pivot point is the left front foot; the left front remains relatively stationary, lifting up and setting down (not swiveling) in place.
- ★ The right front walks a tiny forward half circle around the left front.
- ★ The hind legs walk a half circle around the front legs.
- ★ The left hind crosses over and in front of the right hind.
- ★ Turning on the forehand is an essential suppling, obedience, and positioning (straightening) exercise.
- ★ It teaches the horse to respond to sideways driving and lateral aids.
- ★ Keep this turn very forward. Don't let your horse avoid the aids and back out of the turn.

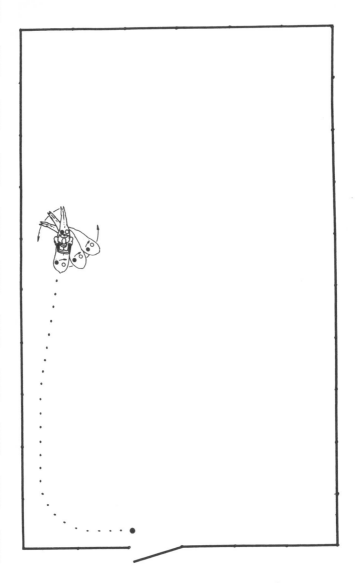

* At the beginning, let him do a walk around, forward turn on the forehand before you require one absolutely in place.
* If a horse backs up, he will be unable to cross over behind and his pivot point will be lost.
* A too-forward turn can be easily counteracted by increasing pressure on the outside (right) rein.

Western Two-Step

- Walk.
- Straight.
- Right corner.
- Straight for one stride.
- Perform the two-step for 3–4 strides to the right.
  - Left seat bone.
  - Left leg behind the cinch and actively pushing sideways each time the left hind lifts and starts a forward/sideways step.
  - Right rein guides direction of travel and prevents bulging right shoulder.
  - Right leg prevents rushing away from the left leg and keeps the horse moving forward.
  - Left rein lightly for slight flexion so horse doesn't overbend to the left.
- Ride straight for a few strides.
- Two-step and repeat.
- After last two-step, change to right bend for the corner.
- Straight.

  The Western two-step can also be performed at jog and lope.

★ This basic lateral movement is sometimes referred to as the "two-track."
★ The line of forward movement is parallel to the arena rail.
★ Teaches the horse to move away from leg while moving forward.
★ Can be used as a prelude to leg yield, sidepass, and turn on the hindquarters.
★ Because of the increased counter flexion, there is an easier chance for the outside shoulder to bulge.

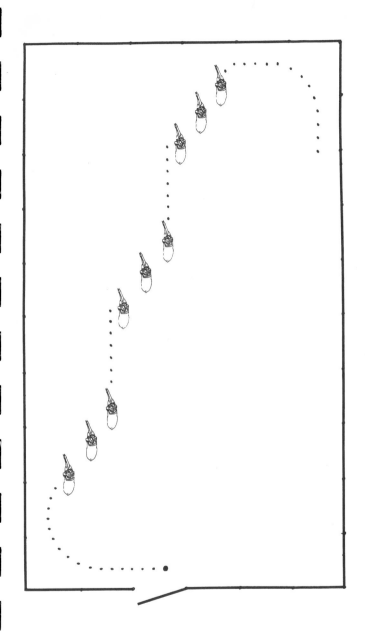

★ It is difficult for a horse to move with this much sideways reach and stay in balance, so be on the lookout for overload: irregular rhythm, rushing, head way down, balking.

Hindquarter Pivot

- Walk around the corner and straight up the long side.
- Check.
- Slight position right.
- Hindquarter pivot.
  - Weight on right seat bone to hold right hind pivot foot down.
  - Lift reins up slightly and back to weight hindquarters and lock pivot foot.
  - Left leg at or slightly in front of the cinch to initiate right turn.
  - Right leg passive but ready to correct or prevent sideways step of the right hind.

When a horse pivots, he ends up on the same track he started.

Don't let the horse back up during the pivot or he will be forced to pick up his pivot foot. There is a fine line between settling the weight *on* the hindquarters and forcing the horse's weight backward *past* the hindquarters.

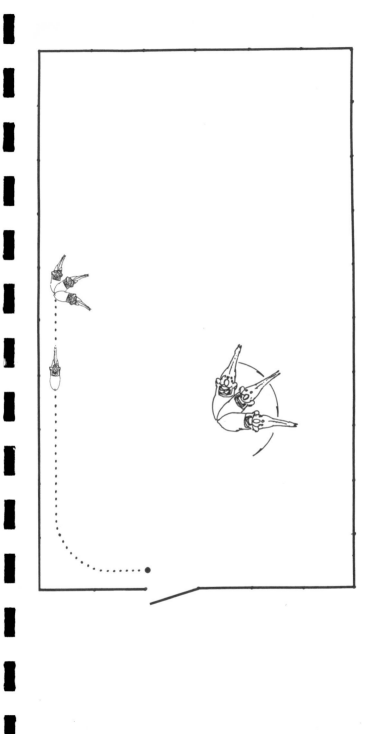

Simple Change Serpentine

- Lope right lead and follow pattern for five-loop serpentine.
- After the first loop, ride straight ahead 20 feet.
- Walk one stride.
- Lope left lead.
- After second loop, ride straight ahead 20 feet.
- Walk one stride.
- Lope right lead.
- Continue until the serpentine pattern is complete.

Variation: Make the simple change through a jog rather than a walk.

Horses can begin to anticipate the downward transition, so vary with other serpentine pattern exercises.

Leave yourself plenty of time and space to straighten in between the old bend (old lead) and new bend (new lead). Maintain the exact serpentine shape. The tendency is to cut across on a diagonal from one loop to another rather than adhere to a very straight line. Be ever vigilant and focus on a post or point across the arena.

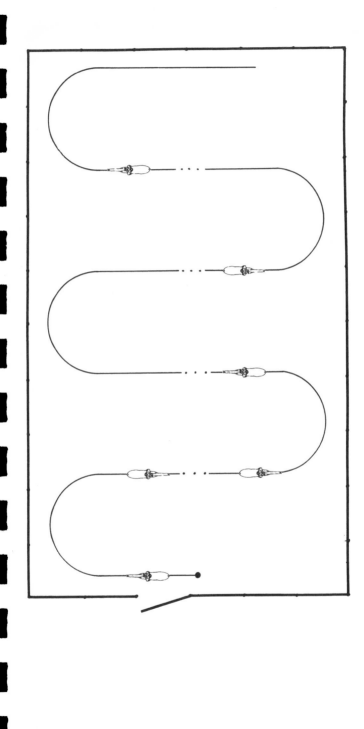

Preparing for Your Test

Work regularly with a qualified instructor.

Practice all the exercises in this guide in both directions.

Visualize the test pattern, "ride" it in your mind. Draw the pattern on a piece of paper several times to be sure you know the order of maneuvers.

Practice individual portions of the test with your horse, but don't over-practice the actual pattern or your horse will anticipate. Anticipation leads to rushed work and errors.

Choose your examiner carefully. You may wish to use your regular instructor or another experienced rider, trainer, or instructor. If you ask someone inexperienced to evaluate you, you'll get unproductive results.

Make photocopies of the score sheet. Since you may want to ride the test several times, have extra copies of the score sheet available.

Arrange to have your test videotaped. Later you can compare the examiner's notes with your actual ride.

Rider warm-up. This is accomplished both in and out of the saddle.

Loosen up by giving your horse a vigorous grooming.

Test your suppleness as you squat down to put on your horse's boots or your spurs. If you are stiff, do some stretches before you mount up.

Once mounted, do a few upper body stretches, arm circles, leg swings, head rolls, ankle rotations, and leg and arm shakes.

Breathe. Throughout your warm-up and your test, be sure you are breathing regularly and properly.

Take air in through your nose, and send it down to fill your abdomen.

Exhale through your mouth to empty lungs and deflate the abdomen.

Especially when you are concentrating and focusing, be sure to breathe in a regular rhythm.

Horse warm-up. Just before the test, warm-up your horse.

Start out at a lazy walk on long reins so your horse can blow and stretch his back and neck and relax.

After a few minutes, sit deep, flex your abdominals, put your lower legs on your horse's sides, and gather up the reins.

For about ten minutes, walk or trot your horse along the arena rail, or make large figures such as 60-foot circles or large serpentines.

Let your horse have a little rest break on a long but not loose rein, as you walk for a minute or two.

Pick your horse back up and practice one or two of the transitions or a lateral or collection exercise from this guide.

Good luck! Ride the test well!

Lope — Halt — 180 — Lope

How to Ride the Test

- Lope right lead.
- Lope right corner with normal bend.
- Lope straight about 60 feet.
- Double intensity check.
- Halt.
- Settle for 1–2 seconds simultaneously introducing...
- Right flexion.
- Perform 180-degree pivot to the right with an active left leg.
- At the same time, change the horse's bend from right through straight to slightly left.
- When you feel the horse securely on the right rein, lope left lead with left bend.

Test Ride Tips

★ When you are loping down the long side, check lightly with every stride.

★ At the moment you are finishing the 180 and getting ready to lope, you are in essence going from a right turn with slight right position to a mini-leg yield to the right with left flexion to a slight left bend traveling straight ahead.

★ When facing the opposite direction, continue using the left leg actively until you feel the horse's left hind leg step sideways toward the rail.

★ The horse is then in position to push off with the right hind for the lope left lead.

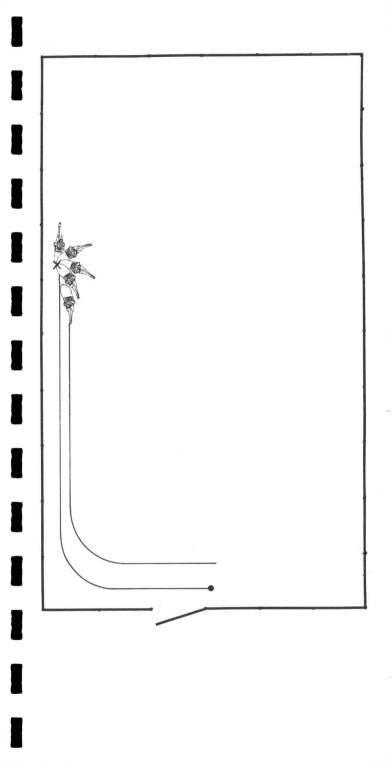

To the Examiner ...

You are performing an important role for the rider you are observing. Please study the test pattern carefully and know the exact instructions. Always strive to encourage, not discourage, a rider by your comments. Look for details that can help a rider improve. Try to determine whether it is the rider that needs help or if it is the horse that needs work.

The Numbers. *High scores:* There are so many things that can be improved in a horse or rider. If you give high scores right away, there is less room for improvement. *Low scores:* When you must give a very low score, offer at least one positive comment along with your suggestions for improvement.

Each maneuver is scored on a basis of 0–10

10 = excellent, perfect, took my breath away!

 9 = everything was correct but lacked exquisite smoothness and brilliance

 8 = good job, everything required was performed but overall it lacked finesse

 7 = average job, performed correctly but lacked absolute smoothness, promptness, accuracy, evenness

 6 = minor mistake such as horse bent incorrectly for a few strides or late transition

 5 = one major mistake such as breaking gait for a few strides but then corrected, wrong lead for a few strides but then corrected

 4 = two major mistakes made that were corrected

 3 = three major mistakes made that were corrected

 2 = one major mistake that wasn't corrected

 1 = maneuver did not resemble test requirements

 0 = didn't perform the maneuver

Comments. Be descriptive and creative with your comments — they will help the rider more than numbers because your words will stay in her mind. If you write "poor jog," it doesn't tell much, whereas "a stumble, quick rhythm at beginning of circle, hollow back and short stride" tells the rider much more.

Score Sheet: Intermediate Western

MOVEMENT	SCORE	COMMENTS
Lope right lead		
Lope right corner		
Lope straight 60 feet		
Check		
Halt		
Settle for 1–2 seconds		
Right flexion		
180-degree pivot to right		
Change bend from right to left		
Lope left lead		

TOTAL

90–100	It's time to move on to Advanced Western.
80–89	Work more on the areas your examiner identified, then retest in about a week.
70–79	Plan to work for several weeks on lope departs, flexion, rhythm, and precise pivots. Then retest.
60–69	Ask your instructor for specific help. Relax, breathe, focus.
50–59	Review all of the exercises in Beginning and Intermediate Western.
0–49	Are you working regularly with a qualified instructor? Is your horse adequately trained?

Other Storey Titles You Will Enjoy

Arena Pocket Guides, by Cherry Hill. Covering both Western and English riding, this six-book series provides illustrated arena exercises and advice for beginners, intermediates, and advanced riders. 32 pages each. Paperback. *Beginning Western Exercises* ISBN 1-58017-045-5, *Intermediate Western Exercises* ISBN 1-58017-046-3, *Advanced Western Exercises* ISBN 1-58017-047-1, *Beginning English Exercises* ISBN 1-58017-044-7, *Intermediate English Exercises* ISBN 1-58017-042-0, *Advanced English Exercises* ISBN 1-58017-043-9.

The Basics of Western Riding, by Charlene Strickland. Covers the Western horse and horse handling, the Western saddle seat, Western tack, becoming a horseman, and trail riding. 160 pages. Paperback. ISBN 1-58017-030-7.

Competing in Western Shows & Events, by Charlene Strickland. Describes Western horse show basics, the show rules and players, showing intermediate riders, showing working horses, timed events, and arena contests. 144 pages. Paperback. ISBN 1-58017-031-5.

From the Center of the Ring, by Cherry Hill. Covers all aspects of equestrian competition, both English and Western. 192 pages. Paperback. ISBN 0-88266-494-8.

Horse Health Care: A Step-by-Step Photographic Guide, by Cherry Hill. Includes more than 300 close-up photographs and exact instructions explaining bandaging, giving shots, examining teeth, deworming, preventive care, and many other horsekeeping skills. 160 pages. Paperback. ISBN 0-88266-955-9.

Horse Handling & Grooming: A Step-by-Step Photographic Guide, by Cherry Hill. Contains hundreds of close-up photographs for feeding, haltering, tying, grooming, braiding, and blanketing. 160 pages. Paperback. ISBN 0-88266-956-7.

Horsekeeping on a Small Acreage, by Cherry Hill. Focuses on the essentials for designing safe and functional facilities on small areas of land. 196 pages. Paperback. ISBN 0-88266-596-0.

Safe Horse, Safe Rider: A Young Rider's Guide to Responsible Horsekeeping, by Jessie Haas. Beginning with understanding the horse and ending with competitions, includes chapters on horse body language, pastures, catching, and grooming. 160 pages. Paperback. ISBN 0-88266-700-9.

These and other Storey books are available at your bookstore, farm store, garden center, or directly from Storey Books, 210 MASS MoCA Way, North Adams, MA 01247, or by calling 1-800-441-5700. www.storey.com.